Celtic Prayers & Practices

An Inner Journey

Alison,
May your prayers
be blessed
David

Celtic Prayers & Practices

An Inner Journey

David Cole

Anamchara Books

 Originally printed as *The Inner Journey: Practices and Prayers for Christ-Centered Meditation.*

Anamchara Books
Vestal, New York 13850

9 8 7 6 5 4 3 2

ISBN: 978-1-62524-375-1
ebook ISBN: 978-1-62524-104-7

Author: David Cole

Contents

The contemplative's life is a prolonged immersion in the rivers of tranquillity that flow from God out into the whole universe and draws all things back to God.

Thomas Merton

If you persevere unhindered in meditation

and prayer to the blessed Trinity, God will be ever with you.

Saint Ita (5th-century Irish abbess)

Welcome

As I sit here writing this, I am in a room at the Open Gate retreat centre on the Holy Island of Lindisfarne, with some mead beside me and the wind howling outside the window. I have just returned from walking outside, and I am grateful for the comfort this room offers me after the effort of pushing against that relentless wind.

The spiritual life has its own wild weather. Life may feel as though we are struggling through a driving wind like the one outside my window. Simply surviving takes all our effort; when we set ourselves to pray, we find our minds are blank. Our inner selves are in such turmoil that we are helpless to focus on the Divine.

Think of the book in your hands as a room where you can take refuge with a cup of mead. The wild weather will continue outside. But rest a little before you go back out into the windy night on your journey. Take heart here. Refocus. Allow your creativity to be renewed.

Or, to use another metaphor, think of this book as an oasis in the middle of the desert, a well of water where you can be refreshed. This is not your destination, only a place where your inner being can be strengthened so you can continue on the long road that will take you deeper on your journey.

As you dip into the well of this book, I pray you will discover your own self more deeply—the True Self, as the ancient mystics called it, the Divine image within you, which is the real you. The simple words and practices you find here will help you silence your false self, the ego that battles within you to create a shiny image for the world to see. As that false self's chatter is silenced, you will discover, within the stillness, not only your True Self but the great Divine Presence who is both within you and all around you, even in the wildest storms, the driest deserts, and the darkest nights.

Dwell awhile in the words offered here. Focus on their light. Allow them to wash over you, like water. Open yourself to the presence of the Great Divine, sweeping over you. Sense the Spirit's gentle breath in your inner being, even as the world's wild winds still howl. Use these words and practices as a starting point for your soul's flight. Continue on from them with your own words. Find your own flow. Travel further on your unique path with the Great Divine.

The inner journey has great rewards—but the wild storms, dark nights, and stretches of barren desert can't be avoided. That's why this book was written. It offers an oasis where you can be refreshed along the journey—and a lantern or two to carry with you when the nights are dark. Here you will find opportunities to be better equipped for your journey. It's an instruction manual for wayfarers based on wisdom garnered from the Celtic tradition, as well as others who have made this journey too.

If these words and practices help you, then I am honoured to have been with you in this way on your journey.

Grace and peace to you.

David Cole
March 2013

The kingdom of heaven

can be reached from any land.

Saint Samthann (8th-century Irish abbess)

1

Preparation for Meditation

Meditation is simply the practice of quieting the mind—the inner self—using techniques in sitting, breathing, and concentrating. It describes a state of concentrated attention on some object, thought, or word, often by turning the attention inward, but attention outward to music or visual imagery is also a common and useful practice. By focusing our minds, we draw in a sense of the Divine Presence—or, to look at it from a slightly different perspective, we extend our inner senses out to connect with the Divine Spirit around us. Meditation can be used both for personal development and to focus on the Divine mind—and both uses can draw us closer to God, while at the same time enabling us to engage more deeply with the Divine image that dwells within us.

When we invoke the Spirit, we ask the Divine to be present with us. This is particular to spiritual meditation, and even more particular to Christ-centred meditation. As you meditate, you call out, asking that God be with you, inhabiting each element of the atmosphere.

During meditation, you are not asking God to do anything for you except be present with you. You are not seeking blessing for yourself; you are not interceding on behalf of others, lifting up their problems. You are not asking God to reveal anything to you or to change you. You are simply asking that the Divine Presence come and sit with you, rest with you, and guide your heart and mind. You are asking only that the Spirit fill this present moment of space and time.

Here in this quiet space we gain strength for our outer lives. By turning to the inner path, we gain light for the outer voyage as well. But meditation does not just happen by itself. It takes discipline to make it a habit; it takes practice.

Imagine you are out backpacking in that dark and windy storm we described in the last chapter. You're far along on your journey, with no convenient retreat centre or bed-and-breakfast in sight. You know if you don't stop and rest for the night, you'll soon be too tired to go on—but you can't just sit down in the wind and rain, not if you expect your stop to do you any real good.

You need to set up camp first. That means you need to locate a good place to pitch your little tent. You'll need to take certain steps to make sure your camp will be safe and secure. If you are a regular camper, these steps will come almost automatically, but if you're new to backpacking, it will take some thought and effort to get yourself settled.

The ancient Celtic Christians knew that entering

God's presence is not necessarily a supernatural experience beyond our control. They understood that practical, down-to-earth habits can make a space for God to enter our lives. So think of this chapter as your instruction manual for setting up camp to meditate—creating that space where God can enter. Here are basic, practical steps for building a lifelong habit, a place where you can return again and again for rest and renewal.

Place and Setting

First and foremost you need to find a quiet place, either inside or outside. Make sure this is a place with the fewest possible distractions, not somewhere family members or other people will likely be passing through.

If you are going to regularly practice meditation—and I suggest you do—it's helpful to practice in the same place each time. This enables your subconscious to recognise the place and setting as your meditation place. Try not to change from one place to another.

Once you have found this place—whether it's an entire room, a sheltered nook outside, or a corner of a room—you may also find it helpful to set it up as a designated meditation area with a comfortable chair and whatever other "props" you need (a table or desk, candles, stones, a beautiful painting, etc.). These objects will also help you to switch into meditation mode. Ensure also that external distractions are minimised: phones unplugged or switched off, doorbell silenced, e-mail unavailable. Do your best to disable whatever might distract you! This is an important time, as important as any of the external calls on your attention. This is your time to dwell in and with the Divine.

Position

Many forms of meditation require specific physical positions. The meditation practices of Celtic spirituality have no hard-and-fast requirements, but the way you sit can make a huge difference to the quality of your meditation. Here is one simple rule to follow: *Sit in a comfortable position, but one that's not so comfortable you will fall asleep.*

Some good positions are: crossed-legged or kneeling down with your feet pointing out behind you. (Your feet muscles may need to get used to this one, or you may wish to purchase a kneeling stool). In both of these you must make sure that your back is straight. You can also sit in a chair, again making sure you are not going to fall asleep, with your back straight. If the seat is wide enough, you can sit cross-legged on it. Otherwise, your legs should be straight in front of you, with both feet on the floor.

In all these positions, rest your hands in front of you, either on your legs or knees. The positioning of your hands can also help focus what you are doing. For example, you may want to rest your hands palms-down on your knees to symbolise that you have let go of your hold on your life. Or you might want to place them palms-up to demonstrate your openness to the Divine Spirit. One Zen hand position forms a circle with opposite thumb tips touching and fingers resting upon each other. This may help you focus on Divine eternity (the endless circle) and your connection with it.

These are all helpful body positions, but as I said, Christ-centred meditation requires no "right" way for you to sit. I do suggest that you discover what works best for you—and then stick with it.

Breathing

Breathing may seem like the most obvious and natural of activities—but effective meditation depends on correct breathing that helps you relax more deeply and concentrate more precisely. You don't want to spend your entire meditation time constantly interrupted by yawning!

Take a few deep breaths right now, and concentrate on the precise movements of your lungs. You will notice, if you are not out of breath, that your breathing pattern consists of more than just in and out, then in and out, but that there is a natural pause in your breathing pattern. In and out . . . then pause . . . then in and out . . . then pause . . . and so on.

When we breathe in, we take in everything that is around us; then our lungs separate everything we need from the air and we breathe out everything we don't need. In the pause between the two, the body sends all the useful parts of the breath into the blood stream. This moment of rest is where we truly gain the fullness of life. This is what happens during meditation, on the spiritual and psychological levels as much as the physical. We are created as body, soul, and mind, all linked together, and through breathing, we make real the unity of our being Celtic tradition refers to this as "breath praying."

The best way to breathe during meditation is to relax and breathe in deeply through your nose. Do not overdo it. You are not trying to hold your breath; simply fill your lungs to a good capacity. When you breathe out—and for this simple, basic breathing it doesn't really matter if you breathe out through your nose or mouth—do it slowly, slowly enough so that you cannot hear the breath coming out of you. Then let the natural rest in your breathing pattern sit for as long as it needs to before you breathe in again.

Zen meditation has a practice that is simply concentrating on the breaths, counting them in and out. You can either do this as counting the in breaths as 1 and the out breaths as 2, or with the in breaths as the odd numbers and the out breaths as the even numbers up to 10; then start again from 1.

These three basic practices we just described—establishing a good place to meditate, sitting in the right position, and breathing correctly—are the first steps to setting up your "camp." With these, you already have what you need to enjoy deep and fulfilling meditation.

But I want to share three extended meditation practices with you as well, things I find helpful. Think of these as ways to make your meditation camp even more secure and effective.

Atmosphere

Creating an atmosphere—combining sense stimuli—offers your brain additional triggers that will allow you to achieve a quiet, focused state of mind quickly and easily. Although we often think with a dualistic perspective, perceiving our senses and our souls as operating in separate realms, in fact, the Divine works through both, and we can use our five physical senses to help us come into the Divine Presence. There really are no rights and wrongs here; create an atmosphere that works for you, using the elements of sound, scent, and spirit.

You may find that gentle music will help your mental focus. Your concentration will drift naturally in and out of the music, and you may be able to resist mental distractions more easily, allowing you to more readily sense the Divine Presence and the spiritual realm. Pick whatever speaks to you. What's important is that the music not be vocal, so that your concentration is not broken by the temptation to sing along with the words.

Incense is another sense stimulus that has drawn people's attention to the Divine Presence for thousands of years. The ancient Israelites used incense in their worship, and many other spiritual traditions do so as well. Aromas are a good way to fill a meditation space, providing a sensual meditation trigger. Particular aromas can aid concentration in different ways. You may want to try essential oil burners—or you may prefer incense burners, which allow you to see and smell the smoke rising from the burner and filling the room. You see the Spirit's presence, while you breathe in the sweet aroma of the Divine.

Focus

Sensual stimuli can draw our attention inward, but they can also distract us when we sit down to meditate. With practice, we get better at focusing anywhere, regardless of noise and visual distractions, but especially as we're starting out in our practice, we need to find places where there are fewer things to pull our attention away from our meditation. Even in a bare, empty cell, however, our busy minds can offer their own sort of distractions. The problem here is that our thoughts become scattered, random, and unfocused. We want to narrow our attention to a single point.

Having an external visual focal point can help you maintain your inner focus. This could be a lit candle, a cross, a stone in your hand, an icon, or a photograph. As your physical senses focus on this specific thing, your mind becomes more focused as well, and mental distractions are less frequent.

Focal points do not necessarily have to rely on your physical senses, however; alternatively, you could meditate with your eyes closed, focusing on an internal picture. This might be a particular place where you have experienced Divine peace in the past, such as the beach or a spot in the forest or a church sanctuary. The Celtic saints all had favorite outdoor places where they retreated to sense God's presence.

If you can't go to your own special place physically, go there in your imagination. You might imagine the sound of waves lapping on the shore or the wind in the tree branches. With the power of your memory and your imagination (both God-given abilities), you can leave your actual location, wherever that is, and rest your mind in a quiet place far from distractions.

Thoughts

Sooner or later, all meditation must confront what is sometimes called the monkey mind: the constant mental chatter inside our heads that never stops. Thinking is what our brains *do*; it's impossible to turn them off. How can we have peace when our brains are so relentlessly busy?

Many times people try to tackle this dilemma with sheer determination and will power. But when we try to consciously stop thinking, this very act is a thought; now we are thinking about not thinking, and our brains are busier than ever! Since we cannot stop our thoughts, we need to step back from them. While their chatter continues, we gently disengage ourselves. We allow ourselves to simply watch their stream.

Imagine you are standing on a riverbank, gazing at things that float by you on the river. You observe these things without trying to either grab hold of them or push them away. During meditation, your thoughts are the objects floating on the river. When you realize you have become engaged with one of them, simply acknowledge the fact and then let the thought drift on its way again. Let it float away from you on the river as you return your focus to meditation.

Your monkey mind is stubborn. You may wonder if it will ever learn to quiet down. But be patient with yourself. When you first start this practice, you may feel as though you are wasting your time because you spend the entire period of meditation letting go of the thoughts that keep engaging your attention. But as you get more practiced, the time your thoughts take to run to an end will become less and less, until it only takes a very short time.

Do not be discouraged with yourself. All new habits take effort. Even what seem like failed attempts build strength for next time.

Now you have what you need to "set up camp," a place to retreat from life's storms when no other shelter is in sight. When you first pitch a new tent, it may take you time to find the right position so that the seams are in the right place and the pegs hold it properly. You may even have to stop and start again—but the more often you pitch the same tent, the quicker and easier it becomes to get it right.

The next chapters will give you some of the "camping equipment" you need to bring inside your tent. These are all helpful meditation tools, but you may not want or need all of them. It's up to you to pick and choose. Try them out. You'll soon find what works best for you.

Christ be beside me,
Christ be before me,
Christ be behind me,
King of my heart.
Christ be within me,
Christ be below me,

Christ be above me,

never to part.

attributed to Saint Patrick

For God's Message is full of life and power... and it can discern

the secret thoughts and purposes of the heart.

Hebrews 11:12 (Weymouth New Testament)

2

Scripture Meditations

Meditating on sacred words has always been a part of Celtic spirituality. This chapter offers samples from the Judaic-Christian holy text commonly known today as the Bible. The exercises use these examples, but you can also use the same meditation patterns with any other verses from this sacred book.

Meditating upon scripture is described throughout the Bible. Psalm 1 begins by saying that the person who meditates on the word of the

Lord (scripture) is blessed and finds pleasure in full understanding of it, that this person is like a tree planted by streams of living water. As you work through this chapter, you too can open yourself to Divine blessings and pleasure, as you dip into the streams of living water.

Lectio Divina

The practice of *lectio divina*, the ancient art of sacred reading, or meditating upon scripture, can be separated into 5 parts: read, reflect, respond, rest, and relate.

Read the scripture. Find a verse or short section of scripture every day. Read the same verse, or a few verses, over and over. You may find that you want to use the same section for several days in a row. Move on only when you feel ready.

Reflect on what it says. After you have read the passage several times, pause for a few moments.

Think about what the words say: What do they mean to you? Is there any particular part that speaks most to you? Allow, the Divine Presence to speak into your heart.

Respond to the Divine. Talk to the Divine Presence about what you have just read, and what thoughts you had about it. Ask God to teach you from it. You may be surprised at how many different things come to you during the time you spend on a single verse or phrase—or you may find that the same thought sinks more deeply into your heart each time you return to that passage.

Rest in the Divine Presence. At the end of your meditation, let go of all your thoughts. Surrender even the words themselves upon which you have been meditating. Allow yourself to rest silently in Divine love and peace. A mother holding her sleeping baby doesn't need to speak to communicate her love, nor do lovers need to fill every moment with chatter in order to commune with each other. This is the same sort of moment between you and the Divine Spirit, a moment of intimacy and total trust.

Relate what you have read to your life. It is no good reading sacred scripture, even if it speaks to your heart, if you never apply it to the way you live your life. This is not about "trying to be a good"; this is about a living, breathing relationship with the Divine Presence, a relationship that filters past your meditation moments into the way you live your everyday life.

To get you started, apply *lectio divina* to the scripture passages in the following pages. First, *read*. Then, I have supplied *reflection* for each passage, and I have offered questions to help you *respond*. Only you can take the final steps: *rest* and *relate*.

The Lord's Prayer

Our Father in heaven,

Hallowed be Your name.

Your kingdom come.

Your will be done

On earth as it is in heaven.

Give us this day our daily bread.

And forgive us our debts,

As we forgive our debtors.

And do not lead us into temptation,

But deliver us from the evil one.

For Yours is the kingdom and the power

and the glory forever.

Matthew 6:9–13

We have here one of the most famous prayers extracted from the Christian sacred text, the prayer that is said perhaps most often within church gatherings, and one which you may be familiar with from your childhood. In fact, quite possibly you are so familiar with it that you no longer think about the words. When you consider meditating on scripture, these familiar words may never even occur to you as something you might want to use.

You may find hidden treasure within these familiar words. Go slowly through this prayer, pausing often within it to meditate upon what it has to say to you. Use each separate piece as a separate meditation.

I have offered here my thoughts to start your meditation, but you will need to take it further and make it personal. At the end of each section I have provided questions you can use to carry your meditation deeper. Meditation is not meant to be merely an intellectual exercise but a way of exploring our own inner landscapes and as the means for drawing closer to the Divine Presence.

Our Father in heaven. . .

To begin, we address one part of the three-part godhead: the Father. The word affirms our relationship with the Divine, and so here we can pause to meditate on what it means to be a child of the Divine One. We acknowledge that the Divine is exalted, above us, beyond us, yet still close enough to us to address and embrace.

What does it mean to you to be the child of the Divine One?

Hallowed be your name. . .

In Exodus, part of the Hebrew scriptures, God gives ten "words" (often translated "commandments"), one of which is: "Do not misuse, or take lightly the Divine name." It is hallowed. "Hallowed" means to be sacred, special, adored, reverenced. The Divine name was deeply important to the Hebrew people. *Elohim, Adonai, El-Elyon, YHWH* (sometimes pronounced *Yehovah*), and many other names for God, all had special meaning and significance.

How can you hallow the Divine name in your life today?

Your kingdom come. Your will be done on earth as it is in heaven. . . . Yours is the kingdom and the power and the glory forever. These invocations from two parts of the prayer are a deep cry from within us. Our cries rise from our knowledge that our separation from the Divine intrinsically affects our world and us. This plea releases our egos. It shouts from deep within us that we desire Divine control in the world rather than ego-driven human control.

These are courageous statements. To pray them for our world, we must allow them to begin within our own spirits.

What area of your life will you open today to Divine control?

Give us this day our daily bread. . . We know we must at one level use our own intelligence and knowledge, skill and gifts to work for our well-being and physical welfare—but at a deeper level, we understand that the Divine One is in ultimate control. The Divine Presence provides for us each day.

Divine provision does not mean we can sit around doing nothing, waiting for things to fall in our laps. Instead, this sentence acknowledges that we are not in ultimate control of our daily physical needs; a greater power, beyond our control, brings us the nourishment we need. The Hebrew scriptures tell how God provided for the Israelites in the desert by sending manna from heaven. Most us won't wake up to find fresh manna spread across the front lawn—but we can increase our awareness of the Divine Presence in farmers' crops and creatures, the plants and animals that give us our food. In this statement from the Lord's Prayer we find the same sentiments that Native Americans expressed when they honoured the life of the animals they killed for food.

Note too that the prayer is for today only. We are given what we need for the day ahead—but no more. The manna provided to the Israelites in the desert spoiled when they tried to store it for another day, and we cannot always see where tomorrow's meal will come from. (See also Matthew 6:34). We like to make longer-term plans for our provision. Where I am going to get grocery money next week? How am I going to pay the rent or mortgage next month? What am I going to do when my contract runs out next year? But here Jesus reminds us that Divine care and provision is about the present moment. When next week, next month, next year comes, the Divine will be there too—but we are called to be fully present in *this* moment, in the Now.

Are you most in need of spiritual sustenance today—or physical? What worries for your well-being are with you today? Can you release them into the Divine hands?

Forgive us our debts as we forgive our debtors. . .

Forgiveness is perhaps one of the hardest parts of life. Sometimes, though, we have a faulty understanding of what forgiveness asks of us. Meditate on these statements, until you understand what forgiveness is *not*.

> Forgiveness is not the acceptance of another's negative hurtful behaviour.
>
> Forgiveness is not saying, "It doesn't matter" —because it often does.
>
> Forgiveness is not to forget, but to say that this will not affect our relationship from this time forward.
>
> Forgiveness is not the same as healing; forgiveness is a choice, which can be instantaneous, but hurts and wounds will take time to heal.

And now meditate on what forgiveness *is:*

> Forgiveness lets go of grudges. It releases injuries done to us into the Divine Presence instead of harbouring them within our hearts.

This letting go is what keeps injuries from festering in our inner selves. As the mystic poet William Blake said in his poem "A Poison Tree":

I was angry with a friend,

I told my wrath, my wrath did end.

I was angry with a foe,

I told it not, my wrath did grow.

As the title of Blake's poem suggests, unforgiveness is a poison to our inner selves, a poison that grows and sends out branches if it is not dealt with appropriately.

Who do you need to forgive today?

Is there any "poison" that you're harbouring in your heart?

Can you choose to let it go?

Do not lead us into temptation, but deliver us from evil. . .

This is a powerful line that acknowledges Divine authority over the powers of spiritual darkness and the evils of the world. The Judaic-Christian scriptures never indicate that God is in the habit of removing folk from dangers and difficulties (see, for example, Daniel 3:19–27, 6:1–22), but these same scriptures are full of examples where God goes *with* human beings through all their problems. "I will never leave you nor forsake you or forget you," says the Divine One (Hebrews 13:5).

You might want to extend your meditation on this by including Hebrews 2:14–15 and 1 John 3:8.

In what areas of your life do you need Divine deliverance today?

The Jesus Prayer

Lord Jesus Christ, Son of God,

have mercy on me, a sinner.

The sentiments of this prayer can be extracted from various places in the Christian scripture. In Luke 18:13, for example, an unnamed man prays in the Temple, "God, have mercy on me, a sinner." In Matthew 20:30, two blind men are sitting by the roadside, and when they hear that Jesus is going by, they shout, "Lord, Son of David, have mercy on us!" By meditating on these words from others' mouths, we can make them our own.

To begin, we make the statement that Jesus is our Lord, the one to whom we commit ourselves, the one to whom our life belongs.

We also make the statement that he is the Christ, the Messiah and the Son of God, the Divinely anointed and appointed one sent to reconcile all created things back to their rightful places, interwoven with the Divine.

What does this all mean to you?

The cry for mercy is one that runs deeply contrary to our egos, our need to posture and impress others. To ask for mercy is to acknowledge that we are the weaker of the parties, to admit and accept that we need the other—here the Great Other—to choose not to exert power over us. It is a cry from within our weakness. It is a cry of humility.

What does this all mean to you?

The prayer ends with the admission that we have fallen short; that we do not match up with our highest potential; that we have failed; that we are "sinners"—people whose egos drive a wedge between ourselves and the Divine One who always seeks to be reconciled with us.

What does this all mean to you?

Divine mercy clears the false colours of our self-inflated egos. This is one of the works the

Cosmic Christ accomplished on the cross. Mercy is the Divine hand stretched out towards us. But we can only be reconnected with the Divine Presence if we reach out our own hand in response. That is what this prayer does. It puts our hands in God's hand, which is already there, waiting.

Extend your meditation on this to include 1 John 1:8–9. And then again, ask yourself:

What does this all mean to you?

John 3:30

He must become greater,

I must become less.

This short verse contains wonderful words to repeat as a simple mantra (a word or short phrase that helps us focus). It can be done with visualisation to enhance the affect.

As you say the first half of this verse, visualise the Divine light entering into your being. You may want at the same time to draw your breath inward.

Then, as you say the second half of the verse, exhale and visualise the shadow of the ego leaving your being.

What Divine qualities do you need to inhale today?

What ego qualities do you need to exhale?

Psalm 23

The Lord is my shepherd;

I shall not want.

He makes me lie down in green pastures;

he leads me beside the still waters.

He restores my soul;

He leads me in the paths of righteousness

for His name's sake.

Even though I walk

through the valley of the shadow of death,

I will fear no evil; for You are with me;

Your rod and Your staff comfort me.

You prepare a table before me

in the presence of my enemies;

You anoint my head with oil;

my cup runs over.

Surely goodness and mercy shall follow me

all the days of my life;

And I will dwell in the house of the Lord forever.

This psalm holds greater treasures than we have time or space to examine here. I encourage you to dig deeper into the words of this beautiful and powerful prayer. Here are some parts on which to focus your meditation.

The Lord is my shepherd. . .

A shepherd is one who leads us; the one whom we trust to show us safe paths. When we use this word to name the Divine One, we are expressing our commitment to follow and trust.

Can you imagine the Divine as a shepherd leading you? Picture it in your mind.

What does he say to you as you follow him?

He leads me beside still waters. . .

In Hebraic culture and mythology, bodies of water were the place in which spiritual darkness and evil dwelt; they were the Abyss. The Psalms are full of cries to God to "rescue me from the deep." The surge of waves was a metaphor for the forces of evil that threatened to swamp the poet. When Jesus calmed the storms (Matthew 8:23–27, 14:22–33), he was demonstrating that he had spiritual power not only over physical creation, but also over spiritual darkness and evil. On another occasion he cast out demons (Matthew 8:28–34), which then went into pigs that ran into the water and drowned; this would have made perfect sense to the people of Jesus' day, since the pigs/demons would have been perceived as fleeing back to the Abyss.

So when the Divine Shepherd leads beside quiet or still waters, it's a demonstration of Divine power over evil. It is a metaphor for God's power to keep spiritual darkness stilled and quiet, at bay.

What would it mean in your life if the Divine Shepherd stilled the deep waters?

Even though I walk through the valley of the shadow of death, I will fear no evil; for You are with me; Your rod and Your staff comfort me. . . Even in the depths of our shadow moments, when we feel the farthest from the Divine Presence, the Spirit is still there (see Psalm 139:7–10).

The rod and staff of an Israeli shepherd were two different things. According to G. Christian

Weiss in his book *Insights into Bible Times and Customs,* "The rod is basically a club of about 30 inches in length, usually with a knob on the larger end formed from the 'bulb' at the root of the little tree from which it is made. This knob might be studded with heavy-headed iron nails or even with flint, thus making it a formidable weapon. . . . [The staff] is a kind of walking stick, about 6 feet in length. . . . It is used in aiding the shepherd in walking over rough terrain, climbing hills or clambering over rocks. The word itself signifies a 'stay' or 'support.'. . . A staff with a crook on the end is used by the shepherd to lift a sheep or lamb from a crevice between the dangerous rocks."

What does this understanding of these words say to you?

Do you see the Divine rod bringing comfort to your life?

Where to you see the Divine staff at work?

In *lectio divina*, we open ourselves to the Divine Presence—and then we commit to carrying that Presence back into the everyday, material world. This ancient practice contains within it both moments of quiet contemplation and a call to action. It describes within its form the ascending spiral of meditation, a movement that carries us inwards, to our inner selves and the Divine Presence—and then outwards, with the call to carry the Divine Presence we discover in these quiet private moments out into the physical world, the world of workplaces and households, relationships and conflicts. Meditation has an ongoing spiritual rhythm, a gentle oscillating spiral, which carries us between spiritual receptivity and spiritual activity. We go deep into our inner beings—and there we find energy and inspiration to face the challenge of the outer world.

The fruit of all study is to perceive the eternal word of God reflected in every plant and insect, every bird and animal, and every man and woman.

Saint Ninian (the first to bring the gospel to the Picts in Scotland in the 4th to 5th centuries)

Learn the words of Scripture
and understand their meaning in your soul.

John Scotus Eriugena
(a 9th-century Celtic theologian)

Understand the creation

if you would wish to know the Creator.

For those who wish to know the great deep

must first review the natural world.

Saint Columbanus

(6th-century Celtic missionary to Europe)

3

Nature Meditations

The ancient Celts referred to Nature as the "Second Book" of God. By this they meant that the Divine Presence was revealed in the natural world as much as through sacred scripture. In Bruce Stanley's *Forest Church*, he writes, "Nature is a doorway into the other-than-human world, a place inhabited by more than plants and animals. The natural world reveals secrets about its Creator, and God speaks to us through the wild and untamed world. Nature is sacred space."

We too can find the Divine One revealed through Nature—and just as scripture is a useful tool for meditation, so too can the natural world be. Here are a few suggestions to get you started.

The Rising Sun

Find a place to sit where you can see the sun rise. Make sure you are dressed appropriately for sitting outside comfortably for a while.

As the sun rises, see the darkness flee from its light. See the beauty of the vast array of colours as the light of the rising sun hits the atmosphere: the clouds, the earth, the trees, the rocks and mountains, the city buildings, the sea, the beach—each has its own shades of purples, oranges, yellows, pinks, whites, reds. Bask in this awe-inspiring spectacle.

As the sun rises, let the brightening sky symbolise the inner self and the Divine Light that rises in you afresh each day. Draw your focus inward.

As the Divine Light rises within you, see the darkness flee.

See the beauty of the vast array of "colours" as the Divine Light hits the parts of your inner self: your heart, spirit, and soul. What does the Divine Light reveal within you?

The Setting Sun

Find a place to sit where you can see the sun setting. Be sure you are dressed appropriately for the time of year. You want to be comfortable enough to take some time.

As the sun sets, notice the slow increase of darkness. See the beauty of the vast array of colours as the light begins to fade: deep reds, oranges, purples, deep blues. Watch the sun descend below the horizon.

Within each of us there is what psychologists have called the shadow side, the part we hide from view. Psychologist Carl Jung suggests that we need to own our shadow side, rather than reject it or deny it. St. John of the Cross wrote of his "dark night of the soul" and how essential this type of experience is to our development as maturing spiritual beings.

As the sky darkens, think of your inner self. As the outside light fades, draw your focus inward.

What is your shadow side?

Do you own it—or does it own you?

What might you discover in a dark night of the soul?

Full Moon

In mythology, the moon is the feminine counterpart to the sun's masculinity. In the modern understanding of the Judaic-Christian faith, the feminine side of God seems to be glaringly missing. But if you look just a little below the surface, there she is.

In the Hebrew sacred text, what Christians call the Old Testament of the Bible, the most frequently used word for the Divine Spirit, what modern Christians call the Holy Spirit, is the Hebrew word *Ruach*. Hebrew, just like romance languages such as French and Spanish, has masculine and feminine nouns. *Ruach* is a feminine noun, and in the Hebrew sacred text, the Holy Spirit is most frequently referred to as feminine.

Another allusion to the feminine side of the Judaic-Christian Deity is the Hebrew term *El-Shaddai*. This name is often translated "God Almighty," but one of the root meanings for the word *Shaddai* is "breasted one"—so at its deepest, most primitive meaning, this name for the Divine means "God, the breasted one."

When you look at the moon, it can be a reminder to you of the Divine feminine. Meditate on the great expanse of the full moon: its brightness and its dominance of the sky. Look deeply into it. Open your heart and soul to the gentle and powerful mothering of the Divine One.

There is a mother's heart in the Divine Heart.

What does the moon say to you in each of its phases?

The Wisdom of the Oak Tree

The ancient Celts honoured all trees, but the oak was particularly meaningful. The oak is strong in its stature and roots. It has a sturdy trunk, far-reaching branches, and, like all trees, is obedient to the seasons. Unlike many other trees, however, its roots reach as deep as its branches stretch high.

In your growth in a relationship with the Divine, do you concentrate as much on your depth (on your hidden roots) as you do on your height (the part of you that may impress others)?

Are you as deeply rooted as you are high reaching?

The oak has inner strength. It is what's called a "pioneer tree," a tree that can thrive in rough or hard soil, since its inner strength gives it a greater chance of survival.

When we are healthy, our strength comes from the Divine image within our true selves—but too often we try to draw strength instead from our egos. This may give us a sense of false strength. In a time of crisis, what we supposed was strength may reveal itself as weakness.

How is your inner strength?

Where does it come from?

When you go through rough and hard times, do you have an inner strength that enables you to overcome the trials?

The oak is patient. It is one of the later-leafing trees. In the spring, while other trees are leafing and flowering, it waits graciously and patiently for its time. Sometimes, oaks even leaf twice, once in the late spring or early summer, and then again in late summer or early autumn to generate longer periods of leaf.

Often we too are called to wait. The Divine has plans for us, plans for our flourishing—but in time, Divine time. The Divine Presence moves to the rhythm of eternity, not at the speed of the modern world.

When you see others around you "flourishing," how patient are you?

Can you wait in quiet confidence for your turn "to leaf"?

The oak has simplicity at its heart. The flower is simple: catkins (male) or spikes (female), which draw no attention to themselves in colour or size. Its leaves are simple, and so are its nuts.

When you look at your life, are there areas where you see clutter, an excess of unnecessary things?

Are there ways in which you seek to draw attention to yourself?

Can you accept simplicity as a Divine gift?

The oak grows in a rhythmic cycle and knows its limits. It produces acorns most years, but in years when it has not gained enough energy, it does not. It produces in abundance every seven years, conserving its energy in a rhythmic cycle.

The Divine Presence flows through the natural world in a rhythm. Each living thing has its own unique rhythm, even as it moves to the rhythm of the whole of creation.

Are you aware of your own personal rhythm of rest and creativity?

Can you accept that seasons of your life will not be as visibly productive as others?

Do you know—and respect—your limits?

Right now, are you in a season of high energy and high productivity? Or are you in a season when, for one reason or another, you are being asked to conserve your energy and do a little less?

Is this a season in your life to turn quietly inward—or a season to work actively in the outer world?

The oak is hospitable. Of all trees, the oak houses the largest variety of creatures and other life (like fungi and creeping plants). Its hospitality to many visitors is also of infinite benefit to the tree. Even in death, oak trees continue to nourish the living community around them.

We too are called to be hospitable (Romans 12:13). Are you?

Can Divine hospitality, which welcomes all, be seen in your actions and life?

Do you reflect Divine openness?

The oak lends itself to many uses. Of all the hard woods, the oak is the most versatile, able to be used for many things. It is easily cut and pliable (it bends well)—and yet in all it does, it always keeps its strength. It is also used in a variety of herbal remedies for good health.

The world we live in is constantly changing; nature is designed to develop and evolve. Are you as open to change?

In scripture, our relationship with God is described in organic ways (see John 15:1–8 for one example). Are you versatile?

Are you willing to bend and be pliable in the Divine hand, knowing you will keep your inner strength?

Are you willing to be useful to those around you?

Do you offer yourself to be used to cure the world's ills?

The Eagle

In Celtic tradition, the eagle was the symbol of vision and prophecy. According to some historians, "Voice of the Eagle" was the title given to prophets and seers in ancient Celtic Briton. In one of the Brittonic languages, the phrase "voice of the eagle" was just one word: *Myrddin* or "Merlin."

The eagle is the bird that sees the most clearly and the furthest. It can soar high in the air and see to the ground. In ancient times, people believed the eagle could look directly into the sun without being blinded.

As you meditate on the eagle, feel your soul rise and soar as the eagle does. Let go of your conscious thought and your conscious vision. Allow the Divine to direct the eyes of your heart, your inner eye.

What do your spiritual eyes see as you soar up into the Divine?

(See also the two prayers entitled "The Eye of the Eagle" in chapter 5.)

Summer Solstice

The Celts celebrated the summer solstice as the year's longest day, the day when the darkness is at its least, and the light is at its greatest. Here is a prayer to help you meditate on the meaning of this day in the year's turning wheel.

Great Light, come and illumine and guide us today.

Shine forth with radiance and power

into the darkness that covers this land.

Let not the days of our destruction overcome us,

let not the darkness have its way.

Leave us not to our own evil devices and any unkind way,

but come and shine with brilliance over this land.

Raise us again into that which we have been,

and can be again in you.

Light of the world, shine within me today.

Shine from within me today and all days henceforth.

Let naught but you be indwelling in me,

And naught but you stand out in me.

Great Light, be my guide and hold me fast,

that I may be the light upon a hill that cannot be hidden.

Shine forth from within me, now and ever more.

Winter Solstice

The winter solstice is the celebration on the year's shortest day, the time when the night is the longest and day the shortest. But it is also a celebration of the coming of light, since from this day on, the days gradually get longer and longer. Use this prayer for Mid-Winter's Day as a starting point for your meditation on this marker in the year's cycle.

Warmth of all warmth,

Comforter of all comfort,

Be within me this day.

I would share your warmth with others,

and be to the other that which the Great Other is to me.

Let not the darkness overcome us,

but let the light shine from within

to illumine that which is darkness.

As the darkness stretches its long hand over this land,

let your Light shine forth from within your people,

that none would be left in darkness,

but that instead we will live

in the hope of the coming Light.

Great Light, be my guide.

Hold me fast in this present darkness,

that I may be the fire on a hilltop in this dark time.

Burn within me, now and ever more.

The Equinox (Spring & Autumn)

The Equinox happens twice a year, in the spring and in the autumn. It is the point in the year when the light of the day and the darkness of night are in perfect balance, when they are equal. This is an opportunity to focus on our own need for balance in our lives. So often our lives are in disequilibrium in some way, too much work and not enough rest, too much apathy and not enough activity. Use the following prayer to look into your heart and meditate, so that whatever the imbalance in your life is, it might be revealed.

Divine Creator,

you made the universe to work in perfect balance,

to find equilibrium in its natural rhythm and in you.

May my life reflect that balance.

I bring before you now

all that is within my life that brings imbalance.

Too much . . .

[you finish the rest of the sentence for yourself]

Not enough . . .

[you finish the rest of the sentence]

As the Earth cycles,

and the balance of the light and dark are equal,

draw me to a place of equilibrium in you.

Give your mind to prayer with humility and with great peace.

Saint Ailbe (6th-century Celtic bishop)

4
Celtic-Style Prayers & Meditations

Celtic tradition offers us many prayers and incantations that are useful meditation tools. As a student and teacher of Celtic Christian spirituality, I have soaked myself in this ancient perspective. Here are some of my own original prayers in the Celtic style, offered to you here in the hopes that they may inspire you to go further with this ancient and yet living form of meditation.

The Caim

a prayer of encircling protection

Encircle me, Lord.

Keep peace within, keep turmoil out.

Encircle me, Lord.

Keep love within, keep hatred out.

Encircle me, Lord.

Keep your Light within, keep spiritual darkness out.

Encircle me, Lord.

Keep faith within, keep doubt out.

You can continue with this prayer yourself by placing whatever you want or is relevant "within" and its opposite "out." An example might be, "Keep calm within, keep tension out"; or, "Keep health within, keep sickness out."

The Cross & Resurrection

a prayer of renewal and a new start

Lord of endless inspiration,
who keeps the seasons turning and creation renewed,
plant in me a renewal of life,
as I leave my past behind,
and look forward to what is to come.
Give me the boldness to step out into the future,
knowing that you hold all things in your hand
as I walk the path you lay before me.
May my past not affect me.
May I stand in your righteousness,
and move forward
wrapped in the knowledge of a clean heart
and a clear conscience.

The Eye of the Eagle (1)

a prayer of vision

Open my eyes,

that I may see the wonder of you in all things, Lord.

Open my eyes to the things of heaven

and the spiritual realm.

Give me vision to see clearly

what you have for me,

a clear vision of the path that you set before me,

that I may follow you in all I do.

Give me the eye of the eagle,

that I may see further, more clearly,

and to be able to look directly

into the Sun of Righteousness.

The Eye of the Eagle (2)

a prayer of vision

As the eagle flies the highest
and sees the furthest of any bird,
may I, Lord, soar high in your presence
and see further into you.
May I know your wind beneath my wings,
lifting me above the trials and troubles I face.
May I have the single eye that focuses on you,
and in so doing is not distracted
by all else that goes on about me.
May the eagle be an inspiration to me,
enabling me to get closer to you,
to see what you see,
and to know what you know.

The Forest Deer

a prayer of peace and calm

Lord of all peace,

who calmed the storms of the seas,

bring calm to my soul,

engulf me in your peace,

which is beyond my understanding,

that I may feel safe from the wilds of this world

and from those of the spirit realm.

Prince of Peace,

come reign in me

with the peace only you can bring,

the peace that draws me

to a state of inner bliss with myself,

with the world around me,

and with you.

Keep me from panic and irrational fear;

keep me from anxiety and worry;

keep me from dwelling on negativity.

Stay my soul with your steadfast security.

Keep me calm and at peace.

The Gateway

a prayer of transition

As I move through this stage in life,

leaving the past to start anew,

I pray your guidance and protection

on all I am and have to do.

Take all fear from within my soul

as I make this transition with you,

as I take the path you have laid before me.

I pass through this gateway with confidence

that on life's journey I have you

with me as my guide.

So keep within me, through changes all,

clear sight of you and of your call.

The Journey

a prayer of pilgrimage through life

As I journey on my way,

Lord, journey with me on life's path,

through forest glades and open meadows,

through valleys dark and mountains hard to climb,

as sunrise brightens and warms my face,

and moonlight shines through night's dark shade.

Guide me in all the storms,

and through all the stillness,

be my companion on this path I tread.

As I journey on through life

and make my way home to your house,

I know, Lord, you are by my side.

Kindle the Flame

a prayer of passion

Lord of the fire,

kindle within me

the passion that drives love,

so that I may live for you with all my strength.

Burn within me with a fire

that consumes my whole being.

Engulf me in your Holy Fire

that falls from heaven

into the centre of my being.

Kindle the flame within my heart, Lord,

that it might ignite others

whose lives touch mine.

The Living Water

a prayer of refreshing

In a dry and barren land

where refreshment for my soul

is sparse and hard to find,

I long for you, Lord.

I thirst for your living water.

May it flow from the wellspring of heaven

into the very depths of my being.

Refresh my soul and revive my life.

As the rains revive the land's plants,

so to you I look to revive my life

with your living water from heaven.

Quench my thirst, I pray.

The Mountain

a prayer of security

As a mountain is firm beneath my feet,

so you, Lord, are a firm foundation.

My soul can rest in the security of you.

As the mountain goat finds surety

in the mountain beneath its foot,

so I find surety in you

You alone are my life's foundation.

On nothing else do I trust my foot to fall.

On nothing else do I establish my life.

Nothing is as secure as you, my Lord,

my God, my Rock.

The Wild Goose

a prayer of freedom

Wild Goose, Holy Spirit of God,

release my life. Free my shackled heart.

Give me freedom to fly with you.

To love and to live in such fullness

that sky cannot be enough to hold me,

nor the highest heavens be too far to reach.

Eternal God of endless flight,

may I rise with you in freedom,

through the death and resurrection of Truth and Life,

Love and Son.

Give me a restored life,

both with the Divine and with humanity.

May I live in the freedom you offer, truly accepting it.

Dawn

a morning prayer

Father of creation,

High King of heaven,

Great Spirit of counsel,

Almighty Three-in-One,

I give this day into your hands.

All that it is, all that it holds,

and all that it will be,

I give it to you

All the stresses and strains,

trials and tribulations

that come my way,

I give them to you,

that I would take on none of them.

All the honour and worth,

praise and glory that would come my way,

I give them to you,

that I would take on none of them.

Keep my feet on the path you have set before me,

so that this day you ordained for me

before I was ever born

will be fulfilled

May your word be a lamp to my feet

and a light to my path today.

Day

a midday prayer

You are at the centre of my life,

my being, my existence.

Draw my thoughts away from the things of the world

as I allow them to be drawn into you.

As the sun rises to its highest point in the sky,

may I lift you to the highest point in my life,

so that the Sun of Righteousness will rise

with healing in his wings,

and bring me deep inner healing.

May you always be

the centre of my being

and the source of my life.

Dusk

an evening prayer

As the sun begins to sink lower in the sky,

and the day begins to wane,

may I be fully aware, King of the universe,

that never does the strength of your love wane from me.

As the Earth turns in its natural cycle of day to night,

may I become aware of all within my inner world

that causes me to turn my back on you,

losing sight of your Divine Light.

May I know your presence

even when your Light seems to fade.

May I rest in the knowledge

that you, Lord, will shine forever.

Dark

a night prayer

In the darkness I turn to you.

In the shadow I turn to you.

As the darkness of the night surrounds me,

may I become aware of the dark night of my soul,

and the shadow within me.

Almighty God, bring me to the morning,

that I would know the rising light again.

Bring me to the dawning within my soul,

that I would know the rising of your Light

again within me.

Let me not despair

when I find myself in the darkness within myself,

but remind me that "even there you are also."

May I know your hand upon me,

drawing me always to the Light.

Notes:

The Sun of Righteousness is a prophetic name for the Messiah, Christ, found in Malachi 4:2. The Wild Goose is seen as the Celtic symbol of the Holy Spirit. See Psalm 139:8, 11–12 to read the reference for "even there you are also."

Do not practice long, drawn-out devotions,

but give yourself to prayer at intervals,

as you would to food.

Saint Comgall (6th-century Celtic abbot)

5
Meditation Words

Just as a visual focal point can help us focus our minds during meditation, words can be used as focal points too. Our monkey brains are silenced when we give them a sentence or two, a short phrase, or even a single word on which to direct their attention.

Meditation Statements

In *lectio divina*, you focus on scripture as a meditation tool. The following statements can all be used in a similar way. These short sentences are offered as examples, but you may find other phrases that speak to you. Statements such as these can be used in meditation during your quiet alone time, but they can also be effective tools for bringing meditation into your daily routine. You may want to stick with the same phrase for a few days or even a few weeks, until you feel you are ready to move on to something else. Sometimes, you may find that the same meditation phrase continues to speak to you for months or even years.

As you repeat these phrases often enough, they become habitual. They may even become your mind's default, something that runs through your head during any small empty space during your day, such as when you're waiting on hold on the telephone, standing in line at the bank or store, or sitting in your car in slow-moving traffic. Almost unaware, you will find you begin to change in response to the slow permeation of these words through your mind and heart.

If we do not let the Spirit flow out from us,
then it will become a stagnant pool within us.

Many of us go through life
pretending to be someone else.
But those who go through life
pretending to be themselves
have the hardest time.

How you see determines what you perceive;
what you perceive determines
how you feel about what you see;
the feelings you have determine
how you see what you see.
Only when we accept who we truly are
can we begin to change who we are.

For as long as you pretend to be someone you are not,
you will be unable to become
the person you really want to be.

Theology without personal experience
is merely intellectual philosophy.
Not until you have experienced the Divine for yourself
does your theology become real and authentic.

The spiritual path truly trod is not a safe place.
It is wondrous and full of adventure,
but it's not for the timid.

Silence is the stillness
in which we hear the most.

The past cannot be changed,
and it has formed us into who we are today.
But it does not have the right to command our future,
nor who we will become.

Love will only be truly found
when the inner eyes see
before the outer eyes cause the mind to judge.

It is important, for the sake of your true self,
your inner being,
that you identify yourself not by what you do,
but by who you are.
Who are you?

To follow God is a journey
of enlightenment and change.

The less I want the less I need.

Mantras

Sometimes, even short meditation phrases may be too long for your busy life. If that's the case, a single word can become an automatic prayer that will restore your sense of God's presence.

For hundreds, perhaps even thousands of years, people have been using "mantras" to help focus their thoughts and hearts. A mantra is simply repeating a single word or very short phrase to help you to maintain your focus during meditation.

In the fourteenth century, the unknown author of the great mystical work *The Cloud of Unknowing* wrote that a one-word prayer "pierces heaven far more swiftly than a whole set of mumbled psalms . . . just as someone in a burning building would simply shout 'help' or 'fire' from the depths of their being." He continued, "The way to pray is that which compresses your whole being in the simplicity of one syllable."

An example of this is the word *maranatha*, the Aramaic word for, "Come, Lord." This word flows easily from the tongue, and it becomes habitual the more often you repeat it. Practice saying this during your meditation times—but then continue to say it each morning as you get out of bed, each day as you go out the door, each time you open your computer, every time you begin any new activity throughout your day, and each night before you fall asleep. By doing this, you are inviting the Divine presence into everything you do.

Here are other mantras you might try:

You are here, Lord.

I adore you.

Into your hands, Lord.

I am yours.

This too is yours.

Your mercy endures forever.

Alleluia.

I am open.

Peace.

Love.

No one would know how to rise
to heights of virtue and contemplation
if he were not first fed
by tokens of sensible things.
John Scotus Eriugena (9th-century Celtic theologian)

The Celtic approach to God opens up a world
in which nothing is too common to be exalted
and nothing is so exalted
that it cannot be made common.
Esther De Waal (modern-day Celtic author and scholar)

6

Mindfulness Exercises

Mindfulness is powerful. It changes our perspectives on life. Research studies have shown that mindfulness meditation can even change the activity of our brain circuits, making more space in our neurons for empathy and compassion, while pushing out anger, anxiety, and violence.

But what exactly *is* mindfulness? Definitions vary. Some describe mindfulness as simply being present in the moment. Others indicate that it's an intense attunement, like a mother's awareness of her baby. For some it is a religious experience, and for others, it's merely a form of heightened consciousness.

In Dan Siegel's *The Mindful Brain,* he lists some other elements of mindfulness:

- an open, curious, nonjudgmental attitude
- focused attention
- nonreactive to inner experiences (you notice your emotions but you do not identify with them)

Perhaps it's most helpful to consider mindfulness as some combination of all these elements. Bring that understanding to the following exercises and consider making them a part of your daily life.

The Power of a Smile

Our initial thoughts on waking easily dominate the entire day. Too often, those thoughts may be negative, and because of them, we have a bad day. The Apostle Paul tells us to "take captive every thought to make it obedient to Christ" (2 Cor. 10:5), and this exercise will help you capture your unruly thoughts.

When you wake each morning, before any other thoughts enter your head, smile. To remind yourself, you might want to put a reminder somewhere, even if it's something as simple as piece of paper with a smiley face drawn on it taped to the ceiling above your head, so that you smile before any other thoughts enter your mind. Focus your thoughts on the smile. Feel it on your face, and also in your heart. Hold this smile for a few deep slow breaths.

Continue to smile throughout your day at various intervals. Each time, hold the smile for just a few deep slow breathes. If you come across a moment in your day when you notice you are becoming irritated, immediately bring a smile to your face. Focus your thoughts and inner self upon the smile for a few deep slow breaths.

You may be surprised at the results!

Letting Go While Lying Down

Take some time to create a time where you will not be disturbed. Lie on your back flat on the floor. Place your arms by your side and relax. If you need a cushion for your head, use only a small thin one. Begin by slowing your breathing and deepening your breaths (but not *too* deep, just slow and easy).

Now feel the floor beneath you. Draw your focus onto the floor and your connection to it. Feel your whole body sink into the floor as your muscles and inner self relax and sink more deeply, as if the floor were a soft piece of silk beneath you.

Picture yourself as a pebble sinking slowly through water from the surface to the water's bed. There is no resistance as you fall, just the water sliding over you as you sink more and more deeply. Continue your focus on the sinking pebble until in your inner eye it comes to a gentle rest on the soft water bed.

Continue to focus on the resting pebble as you breathe slowly and deeply.

When you "come out" of this mindfulness meditation, draw yourself together slowly and get up gently and carefully.

Walking in Rhythm with Your Breath

Do this mindfulness exercise when you have time to walk slowly.

Gradually, as you walk, bring your steps in time with your breath.

Slow your steps and breathing slightly, but not too much.

Walk like this for some time.

Compassion for the Person You Dislike or Despise the Most

Jesus tells us to "love our enemies and pray for those who stand against us" (Matthew 5:44). This may seem hard to do: to love and pray on behalf of someone who has hurt us, someone we resent, maybe even despise. This mindfulness meditation is designed to help us begin the journey down the path of loving our enemies.

Sit quietly in a place where you will not be disturbed. Close your eyes and bring an easy smile to your face. Picture in your mind's eye the images of people who have caused you hurt or people whom you are struggling to like and accept.

For a moment, draw to mind that which has caused you these feelings about these people. What is it that you dislike, even hate, about these individuals?

Now contemplate what makes these people happy, what brings them joy, and what brings them pain and suffering in their everyday lives.

Contemplate their perceptions of the world and of life. Try to see what patterns of thought and reasoning they follow. Examine what motivates their actions.

Finally, contemplate their very consciousness. Have prejudices, narrow-mindedness, and fear influenced their views and what they think? Has hurt caused their actions toward you? Perhaps others have shown them anger and hatred. Consider whether these people are in control of their inner selves—or whether they are controlled by circumstances and fear.

Continue to consider the deeper aspects of these people until you feel compassion—until you feel a sense of warmth rising within your inner self, like a well of fresh spring water, renewing the way you feel and think.

Practice this exercise many times, focusing on the same people, until the well of compassion turns to continuing love.

Letting Go of the Things You Fear to Lose

We all have things we hold dear to us, things we fear to lose. But for us to be truly free within ourselves—and for us to be truly and deeply connected to the Divine—we must let go of these things in our consciousness so that they are not part of our psychological foundation but a part of our growth. If they *are* part of our foundations, then, if we do lose them, we will be shaken to our very cores. Letting go of the things we fear to lose does not mean actually losing them; it simply means resting them in the Divine hands, placing them before God, and leaving them to Divine control, accepting that the Divine plan may want different things of them than we do.

Sit quietly and still in a place where you will not be disturbed. Close your eyes and draw to mind those things you fear to lose.

Picture them each one by one: people, animals, possessions, places. Focus on why they are so important to you.

Draw a small smile to your face as these precious things pass through your conscious thought. Be thankful that you have these things, and that they mean so much to you.

Now picture yourself holding these things within your hands. Real-life perspective is unimportant here; so, for example, if you are thinking of a person, picture that individual small enough to fit within your hands.

Now picture the image of the Divine—whatever that is for you—in front of you. In your mind's eye, step forward, bow your head, and stretch out your arms with these things in your hands. Open your hands and place these precious things within the Divine.

Do not leave yet, but picture these precious things enclosed by the Divine Spirit. Know that God loves these things also, and that the Divine One has a plan for each of them, both within your life and separate from you.

Now leave this image, without taking hold of that which you have placed within the Divine. Leave it there. Let it go. In your mind, walk away without it.

Within your mind's eye, contemplate the meaning of what you have just done. These things you have placed within the Divine are still physically with you, but you no longer hold them in the foundations of your inner self. They continue to be a part of your existence, but they are held now within the Divine. They do not mean any less to you, but you have let them go.

You never really possess things.
You merely hold them for a while.
But if you are unable to let them go,
you are held by them.
Anthony de Mello

Letting Go of Hurt and Resentment

Many of us hold on to hurt and resentment. We brood over them. We allow them to control our thoughts and emotions. We keep them fresh, when it is way past time for them to heal.

We all get hurt, emotionally and spiritually. Hurt is normal, and we need to allow ourselves a time of pain and grieving, followed by healing, just as we do when we break a leg or suffer some other physical pain or accident. If instead we become comfortable with our pain, or we find that is useful in some way—perhaps for manipulating others or for giving ourselves an excuse for not trying new things—then the wound begins to fester. Like a physical sore on the skin, if we continually pick at it, it will become infected and gangrenous. It might even kill us in the end. To prevent that, we need to clean out any infection within our souls. Otherwise, these ancient emotional scars may become so dark and gnarled and twisted that they strangle our inner lives.

You may need to have the company of trusted friends following this exercise, so make sure you have them near before you begin.

Sit quietly and still in a place where you will not be disturbed. Close your eyes and breathe slowly and deeply.

Draw to mind the hurts and wounds you hold within your inner self. Consider whether you have completed the grieving process for these things, or if you have held on to them beyond what is good for your soul.

If you feel you have not completed the healing process of these things because these things are truly still too new and current, then simply set them aside for now. Give yourself time to heal. This exercise is not for those things, but only for those wounds that have lingered far too long.

Now focus on to these old hurts. Consider what it was that caused you this hurt and pain in the first place. Draw to your heart the feelings you felt. Be sure to concentrate only on your emotions rather than trying to intellectualise or rationalise your hurt and resentment. Simply begin to feel what you felt when you first suffered this wound.

Now begin to picture this hurt as a physical wound, perhaps like a cut on your skin.

Picture the wound healing, like a speeded-up film. Open yourself to the feelings you experience. Remember how a cut on your skin feels as it heals—and now imagine your heart going through the same process.

Sense the Divine presence surrounding you like a cloak, wrapping you, holding you. Within this cloak is healing—Divine healing—of your inner pain. In this cloak is safety and security.

This Divine cloak can fill the infected holes left in your heart. You no longer need those ancient wounds to define you. You can let them heal, because you are safe within the surrounding presence of the Divine, wrapped up, close and secure. Here you can find wholeness. You discover a healthier identity that can let go of the past.

Follow this exercise for each wound you recognized, each hurt and resentment you have harboured.

God to enfold me,
God to surround me.
ancient Celtic prayer

Deep peace of the running wave to you.
Deep peace of the flowing air to you.
Deep peace of the quiet earth to you.
Deep peace of the shining stars to you.
Deep peace of the infinite peace to you.
ancient Celtic prayer

CONCLUSION

The ancient Celts knew that the inner journey is a long one. We may begin it over and over—but it never ends, at least not in this life. Along the way, meditation offers moments of renewal, as well as the practical equipment we need for the journey. Meditation gives us both solace and new energy. It is a resting spot along the inner journey, and at the same time, it is the path itself.

As you make meditation a regular part of your life, you will discover you are not the self others assume you are; neither are you defined by what you have become due to your life circumstances and experiences. Meditation will help you find who you really are, your true self, your deep inner being.

Use this book as your guidebook. Leave behind the external projection of your self that you've created to please others—and discover instead the Divine image that is the light in the centre of your being. With the ancient Celtic saints, set out on the inner journey.

Be Thou my Vision, O Lord of my heart;
Naught be all else to me, save that Thou art.
Thou my best Thought, by day or by night,
Waking or sleeping, Thy presence my light.

Be Thou my Wisdom, and Thou my true Word;
I ever with Thee and Thou with me, Lord;
Heart of my own heart, whatever befall,
Still be my Vision, O Ruler of all.
8th-century Celtic hymn

The Mystic Path of Meditation: Beginning a Christ-Centered Journey
Author: David Cole
Price: US $14.95 | UK £8.99
Paperback
E-book Available
154 pages
ISBN: 978-1-937211-99-8

Explore the Christian theology that underpins meditation—and discover the practical spiritual benefits of this ancient practice.

"Meditation is one of the great treasures of our Christian contemplative tradition, though largely forgotten by modern churches. In this delightful book, David Cole gently invites readers to rediscover this ancient path to deeper relationship with God. David writes with a spirit of ease and joy as he guides us through meditation with scripture, our breath, our bodies, and the natural world. This insightful and accessible book is a welcome addition to the contemplative renewal of our time."

—***Mark Kutolowski***, OblSB, Salva Terra peace pilgrim and founder of New Creation Wilderness Programs

Water from an Ancient Well: Celtic Spirituality for Modern Life

Author: Kenneth McIntosh, M.Div.

Price: $24.95

Paperback

E-book Available

352 pages

ISBN: 978-1-933630-98-4

Discover the world of the ancient Celtic Christians and find practical insights for living in the twenty-first century.

"When I was reading *Water from an Ancient Well*, I sometimes felt like I taking a spiritual pilgrimage to Cano Cristales, the most beautiful river in the world or the river of five colors. Located near the town of La Macarena in Colombia, South America, the river is famous for its colorful blotches of blue, green, black, and red causing some to call it the river that ran away to paradise. If you want to run away to paradise for a couple of days, and drink living water from a source unlike any other, read Kenneth McIntosh's deeply satisfying book." —***Leonard Sweet***, best-selling author and professor.

Earth Afire with God: Celtic Prayers for Ordinary Life

Author: Anamchara Books
Price: $12.95
Paperback
E-book Available
120 pages
ISBN: 978-1-933630-96-0

Here are prayers and blessings to sanctify your daily life. They will remind you to look for the holiness of the everyday; they will show you the real presence of God in Creation. Illumine your life with the ancient Celts' perspective on prayer. Each glimpse we have of the Earth's beauty, each ordinary sound we hear, every bite of food we eat, and even our daily routines, can all reveal God.

Kenneth McIntosh, author of *Water from an Ancient Well, Celtic Spirituality for Modern Life*, writes, "This book knocks the dust off ancient treasures—such as selections from the Carmina Gadelica—and also introduces some lovely new prayers, all written from the Celtic perspective."

77737254R00074

Made in the USA
Columbia, SC
04 October 2017